To those who seek to unravel the intricate web of human perception and persuasion, and to the brave souls who strive for truth amidst the chaos of manipulation, this book is dedicated.

The Psychology of War Propaganda

How It Shapes Public Opinion

Levent Gülkök

TABLE OF CONTENT

Foreword

Chapter I

Chapter II

Chapter III

Chapter IV

Chapter V

Chapter VI

Chapter VII

Chapter VIII

Foreword

Propaganda is a methodical and deliberate attempt to manipulate people's opinions, stations, beliefs, and actions using colorful communication ways. It's a form of persuasion that's also used to impact the public's perception of a particular idea, product, or service.

Propaganda can be set up in colorful fields similar as political propaganda, war propaganda, commercial propaganda, religious propaganda, health propaganda, environmental propaganda, artistic propaganda, agrarian propaganda, educational propaganda, and social media propaganda.

Propaganda is a means of conveying information to sway the opinions, persuasions, and conduct of a particular group of people. It's apparent in different mediums similar as political movements, marketing, and digital platforms. Overall, the study of propaganda is important because it allows us to more understand how dispatches are drafted to impact our stations, beliefs, and actions. By studying propaganda, we can more understand how we're told by the dispatches we encounter in our diurnal lives. Propaganda is a form of communication that aims to affect people's opinions, stations, and conduct. It has been used throughout history by colorful institutions, similar as governments, pots, religious associations, and social movements, to promote their program and gain support from the public.

In the terrain of politics, propaganda is constantly used to sway public opinion in favor of a particular seeker or party. Political propaganda can take numerous forms, similar to crusade adverts , speeches, rallies, and social media posts. It constantly employs emotional prayers, similar to fear, outrage, or advisable, to rally selectors and produce a sense of urgency around a particular issue. Propaganda plays a significant part in shaping public opinion and impacting people's stations and conduct. It can be used for both positive and negative purposes, depending on the intentions of the propagandist. As consumers of propaganda, it's important to be alive of its ways and motives and to critically estimate the information presented to us.

War propaganda is the use of communication ways to impact the public's opinion about war or conflict. War propaganda can be used to promote nationalism, demonize the adversary, or justify military conduct. It's a form of propaganda that's used to justify military action and rally support for a war trouble. By studying war propaganda, we can gain sapience into how governments manipulate public opinion to support their military juggernauts.

War propaganda is another common form of propaganda that's used to justify military action and rally support for a particular conflict. It constantly portrays the adversary as evil or barbaric and portrays one's side as heroic and noble. War propaganda can have a profound impact on public opinion, as it can impact people's amenability to support or oppose military action.

Chapter I

Introduction to War Propaganda

The Definition and History of War Propaganda

Propaganda has long been a powerful tool utilized by nations during times of war to shape public opinion and garner support for military endeavors. In this subchapter, we will delve into the definition and history of war propaganda, shedding light on its origin, evolution, and impact on society.

To begin with, war propaganda can be defined as the deliberate dissemination of information or ideas, often misleading or biased, with the aim of influencing public opinion and swaying individuals towards a particular perspective or course of action during times of armed conflict. By manipulating emotions, beliefs, and values, war propaganda seeks to create a favorable image of one's own nation or military and demonize the enemy.

The roots of war propaganda can be traced back to ancient civilizations, where rulers utilized various forms of communication to rally their populations for war. From the Egyptian pharaohs to the Roman emperors, leaders recognized the power of propaganda in shaping public sentiment and mobilizing their armies. However, it was during the two World Wars of the 20th century that war propaganda truly flourished.

In both World Wars, governments on all sides employed sophisticated propaganda machinery to manipulate public opinion. Mass media, such as newspapers, radio, and later television, became powerful tools in disseminating propaganda messages to millions of people. Governments employed skilled propagandists who crafted persuasive narratives, often resorting to emotional appeals, patriotic symbols, and demonization of the enemy.

During World War I, for instance, governments utilized posters, films, and pamphlets to depict the enemy as barbaric, inhumane, and a threat to civilization. These propaganda efforts aimed to instill fear and hatred towards the adversary, while fostering a sense of unity and nationalism among the population.

In World War II, both the Axis and Allied powers employed propaganda on an unprecedented scale. Nazi Germany, under the leadership of Adolf Hitler, used propaganda to promote anti-Semitic beliefs and justify their aggressive expansion. Meanwhile, the Allied powers utilized propaganda to mobilize their populations, recruit soldiers, and promote the values of freedom and democracy.

Since then, war propaganda has continued to evolve with advancements in technology and the rise of digital media. Today, social media platforms and online news outlets have become battlegrounds for competing propaganda narratives. Governments, terrorist organizations, and even individuals can now disseminate propaganda messages instantly to a global audience, further blurring the lines between truth and manipulation.

Understanding the definition and history of war propaganda is crucial in comprehending its impact on society. By recognizing the techniques and strategies employed by propagandists, individuals can develop a more critical and discerning approach to media consumption, ensuring they are not swayed solely by emotionally charged narratives. In the following chapters, we will explore the psychological mechanisms behind war propaganda and its effects on public opinion, shedding light on how individuals can become more resistant to its manipulative tactics.

The Purpose and Goals of War Propaganda

War propaganda has been a powerful tool used throughout history to shape public opinion and rally support for military actions. This subchapter explores the purpose and goals behind the use of war propaganda, shedding light on the psychological mechanisms that drive its effectiveness.

At its core, war propaganda aims to influence public perception and generate a specific response from the masses. Whether it is to garner support for a war effort, demonize the enemy, or justify military actions, war propaganda serves as a catalyst in shaping public opinion. Understanding its purpose is crucial for people interested in the field of war propaganda.

One of the primary goals of war propaganda is to unify and mobilize the population behind a common cause. By creating a sense of national identity and fostering patriotism, propaganda aims to instill a strong sense of loyalty and commitment among the public. It seeks to create a shared enemy image and convince individuals that their participation in the war effort is not only necessary but also morally right.

Furthermore, war propaganda often aims to dehumanize the enemy and portray them as a threat to national security and values. By emphasizing their flaws, atrocities, and contrasting them with the virtues of one's own side, propaganda seeks to generate fear and hatred towards the enemy, thus justifying military actions and rallying support.

Another important purpose of war propaganda is to manipulate public opinion through the selective presentation of information. Propaganda can distort facts, exaggerate threats, or omit crucial details to create a one-sided narrative that supports the desired objective. By controlling the information flow, propaganda aims to mold public perception and control the discourse surrounding the conflict.

Additionally, war propaganda seeks to maintain morale and minimize dissent within the population. By presenting a positive and optimistic outlook, it aims to boost public morale, prevent doubts or questions about the war effort, and suppress any opposition that may arise. Propaganda often employs emotional appeals, such as heroism, sacrifice, and victory, to keep the population motivated and committed to the cause.

In conclusion, the purpose and goals of war propaganda are multifaceted, aiming to shape public opinion, unify the population, dehumanize the enemy, manipulate information, and maintain morale. By understanding these underlying objectives, people interested in the field of war propaganda can better analyze and critically evaluate the messages presented to them, ensuring a more informed and discerning response.

The Psychology Behind War Propaganda

War propaganda has long been employed as a powerful tool to shape public opinion and rally support for military campaigns. Understanding the psychology behind war propaganda is crucial for anyone interested in the fields of war propaganda and its impact on society. In this subchapter, we will delve into the various psychological mechanisms at play in war propaganda and how they influence individuals and societies.

One of the key psychological factors in war propaganda is fear. Propagandists often exploit people's natural fear of the unknown and the threat of violence to manipulate public opinion. By creating a sense of imminent danger, they can sway individuals to support war efforts and sacrifice personal freedoms for the sake of national security. Fear is a potent emotion that can override rational thinking, making people more susceptible to propaganda messages.

Another crucial aspect of war propaganda is the creation of an "us versus them" mentality. Propagandists aim to foster a strong sense of national identity and unity by emphasizing the differences between "us" (the in-group) and "them" (the out-group). This division serves to dehumanize the enemy and justify acts of aggression. By portraying the enemy as evil, propagandists can manipulate public sentiment and garner support for military action.

Furthermore, war propaganda often relies on cognitive biases and heuristics to influence public opinion. Cognitive biases, such as confirmation bias and the availability heuristic, can lead individuals to selectively process information that aligns with their pre-existing beliefs and perceptions. Propagandists exploit these biases by presenting information that supports their agenda while downplaying or omitting contradictory evidence.

Additionally, emotional appeals play a crucial role in war propaganda. Propagandists use carefully crafted narratives and imagery to evoke strong emotional responses from the audience. By appealing to emotions such as patriotism, pride, or anger, propagandists can sway public sentiment and foster a sense of collective identity that supports military actions.

Understanding the psychology behind war propaganda is essential for critically analyzing and resisting its influence. By recognizing the manipulative tactics employed by propagandists, individuals can develop a more informed and independent perspective on military conflicts. By questioning the narratives presented by authorities, people can strive for a more nuanced understanding of complex geopolitical issues and work towards a more peaceful world.

In conclusion, the psychology behind war propaganda is a fascinating and vital subject. By exploring the various psychological mechanisms at play, we can gain insight into how individuals and societies are influenced by propaganda messages. Armed with this knowledge, we can strive to be more discerning consumers of information and actively resist the manipulation tactics employed by war propagandists.

Chapter II

The Techniques of War Propaganda

Manipulation of Emotions

In the realm of war propaganda, emotions are powerful tools that can be skillfully manipulated to shape public opinion. Understanding the tactics used to harness these emotions is crucial for anyone seeking to grasp the psychology behind war propaganda. This subchapter delves into the various techniques employed to manipulate emotions and their profound impact on the masses.

War propaganda thrives on stirring up strong emotions such as fear, anger, and patriotism. By tapping into these primal feelings, propagandists can easily sway public opinion and rally support for their cause. Fear, for instance, can be used to portray the enemy as a looming threat, instilling a sense of urgency and the need for action. Through carefully crafted narratives, propagandists amplify this fear, creating a climate of anxiety and insecurity.

Anger is another potent emotion that can be effectively harnessed. By highlighting real or perceived injustices committed by the enemy, propagandists fuel anger within the population, channeling it towards a perceived common enemy. This anger can be used to justify military action, painting it as a necessary response to rectify past wrongs.

On the other hand, patriotism is a powerful emotion that can be exploited to rally support for war efforts. Propagandists often manipulate this sentiment by emphasizing national pride, unity, and the defense of one's homeland. By framing the conflict as a battle for national identity and security, they evoke a strong emotional response, encouraging individuals to align themselves with the cause.

It is important to note that the manipulation of emotions in war propaganda is not solely limited to negative feelings. Positive emotions, such as hope and relief, can also be skillfully employed to sway public opinion. Propagandists often present their side as the harbinger of positive change, promising a better future once victory is achieved. This instills hope within the population and fosters support for military action.

By understanding how emotions are manipulated in war propaganda, individuals can become more discerning consumers of information. Recognizing the tactics employed allows for a more critical analysis of the messages presented, encouraging a deeper understanding of the motives behind war propaganda.

In conclusion, the manipulation of emotions is a crucial aspect of war propaganda. Fear, anger, patriotism, and hope are skillfully exploited to shape public opinion and garner support for military actions. By being aware of these tactics, individuals can guard themselves against undue influence and gain a more comprehensive understanding of the psychology behind war propaganda.

Creation of Enemy Stereotypes

In the realm of war propaganda, one of the most potent and effective techniques employed is the creation of enemy stereotypes. These stereotypes play a pivotal role in shaping public opinion and are crucial in mobilizing support for war efforts. By manipulating perceptions and using psychological tactics, war propaganda crafts a distorted image of the enemy, dehumanizing them, and fostering fear and hatred among the masses.

The creation of enemy stereotypes begins with identifying a target population or nation that is perceived as a threat. Through a carefully orchestrated campaign, the propaganda machine then works to construct a negative narrative around this enemy, emphasizing their flaws, exaggerating their aggression, and highlighting their differences from the home population. The objective is to create a sense of "us versus them," fostering a strong national identity and unity among the people.

War propaganda utilizes various mediums to perpetuate these stereotypes. Through newspapers, radio broadcasts, and now social media platforms, carefully crafted messages of fear, suspicion, and demonization are disseminated to the masses. Visual imagery, such as cartoons, posters, and films, also play a significant role in reinforcing these stereotypes, often depicting the enemy as subhuman, barbaric, or even evil.

By creating enemy stereotypes, war propaganda effectively manipulates public opinion and garners support for military actions. Fear and hatred towards the enemy are cultivated, leading to a devaluation of their lives and a justification for violence. The portrayal of the enemy as a threat to national security and core values further fuels the desire for retaliation and justifies the sacrifices made in war.

However, it is essential for people to be aware of the psychological tactics employed by war propaganda. Recognizing the creation of enemy stereotypes allows individuals to critically analyze the information presented to them and question its validity. By understanding how these stereotypes are constructed and perpetuated, one can resist being swayed by propaganda and work towards a more nuanced understanding of the complexities of war.

In conclusion, the creation of enemy stereotypes is a powerful tool in war propaganda. It molds public opinion, fosters fear and hatred, and justifies military actions. However, by being aware of these tactics, individuals can guard themselves against manipulation and strive for a more informed perspective on war. It is imperative for people to critically analyze the narratives presented to them and challenge the stereotypes that perpetuate division and conflict.

Censorship and Control of Information

In the realm of war propaganda, one of the most powerful tools employed by governments and influential entities is the censorship and control of information. This subchapter delves into the intricate dynamics of how such practices shape public opinion and influence the course of conflicts. By shedding light on this crucial aspect, we hope to empower people to critically analyze the information they receive and understand the underlying motives behind the dissemination of propaganda.

Censorship, as a means of controlling information, is often justified by governments as necessary for national security, but it also serves as a powerful tool to manipulate public opinion. By restricting access to certain facts, narratives, or alternative viewpoints, those in power can shape public perception and control the narrative of war. This form of information control makes it easier to mobilize public support for military actions, demonize opponents, and justify controversial policies.

The psychology behind censorship and control of information lies in the human tendency to trust and rely on authority figures and institutions. When governments or influential entities control the information flow, they assume the role of trusted sources, shaping public opinion to suit their objectives. This manipulation often operates subtly, with strategic omissions, biased narratives, or outright falsehoods, all aimed at influencing public sentiment and garnering support for war efforts.

Understanding the mechanisms of censorship and information control is crucial for people interested in war propaganda. By recognizing the tactics employed, individuals can develop a critical mindset, questioning the information they receive and seeking alternative sources. This subchapter explores various historical and contemporary examples, illustrating the far-reaching impact of censorship on public opinion during times of war.

Furthermore, this subchapter examines the implications of censorship and control of information on the ethics of war propaganda. It raises important ethical questions about the responsibility of governments and influential entities in manipulating public perception and influencing the course of conflicts. By encouraging readers to reflect on these ethical considerations, we aim to foster a more informed and discerning audience, better equipped to resist the psychological impact of war propaganda.

Ultimately, the subchapter on censorship and control of information serves as a wake-up call, urging people to question the narratives they encounter in times of conflict. By empowering individuals to challenge the manipulation of information, we hope to mitigate the impact of war propaganda and promote a more informed and critical public discourse.

Dehumanization of the Enemy

Dehumanization of the Enemy: Unveiling the Dark Tactics of War Propaganda

In the realm of war propaganda, one of the most insidious and effective techniques employed is the dehumanization of the enemy. This subchapter aims to shed light on this dark aspect of psychological warfare, exposing how it shapes public opinion and influences our perceptions of those involved in conflicts.

War propaganda, throughout history, has played a pivotal role in swaying public sentiment, rallying support, and justifying military actions. By labeling the enemy as subhuman, evil, or morally corrupt, propagandists seek to manipulate our perceptions, stirring hatred and fear to garner support for war efforts.

The dehumanization process begins by stripping the enemy of their individuality and reducing them to a faceless mass. Through carefully crafted narratives, images, and language, propagandists create a dichotomy – "us versus them" – wherein the enemy is portrayed as a monolithic force devoid of humanity. By emphasizing the differences between "us" and "them," propaganda aims to erode any sense of shared humanity, making it easier for the public to accept violence and aggression against the enemy.

Dehumanization extends beyond mere rhetoric and imagery. It manifests in the form of stereotypes, caricatures, and even outright lies. The enemy is often portrayed as bloodthirsty, barbaric, and lacking in any redeeming qualities. These portrayals perpetuate the notion that the enemy is less deserving of empathy or consideration, making it easier for the public to justify the atrocities committed during times of war.

Through dehumanization, war propaganda attempts to manipulate public opinion by generating fear, anger, and a desire for vengeance. By depicting the enemy as less than human, propagandists appeal to our primal instincts, invoking a sense of self-preservation and a need to protect our own. This emotional manipulation is a powerful tool, as it can override rational thinking and critical analysis.

Understanding the dehumanization tactics employed in war propaganda is crucial for people interested in war propaganda niches. By recognizing these techniques, we can become more discerning consumers of information, questioning the narratives presented to us and seeking a more nuanced understanding of conflicts. Additionally, acknowledging the role of dehumanization in war propaganda can foster empathy and compassion, reminding us of the shared humanity that connects us all.

In conclusion, the dehumanization of the enemy is an essential aspect of war propaganda, influencing public opinion and shaping the perception of those involved in conflicts. By stripping the enemy of their humanity, propagandists aim to generate fear, hatred, and support for military actions. It is vital for people interested in war propaganda niches to be aware of these tactics, enabling them to critically analyze and challenge the narratives presented to them. Ultimately, understanding the dehumanization of the enemy can help us foster empathy and compassion in times of conflict, reminding us of the shared humanity that binds us all.

Utilizing Nationalism and Patriotism

Utilizing Nationalism and Patriotism in War Propaganda

In the realm of war propaganda, one cannot underestimate the power of nationalism and patriotism. These two concepts have been skillfully employed throughout history to shape public opinion and rally support for military endeavors. Understanding how nationalism and patriotism are utilized in war propaganda is crucial for people interested in the field, as it sheds light on the psychological mechanisms at play.

Nationalism, the belief in one's nation and its superiority, is often exploited to garner support for war. Propagandists tap into people's sense of national identity, emphasizing the uniqueness and exceptionalism of their country. By portraying the enemy as a threat to national values, security, or way of life, they stoke fear and anger, thereby strengthening the collective resolve to fight.

Patriotism, on the other hand, is the love and loyalty towards one's country. It is harnessed by war propagandists to evoke a sense of duty and sacrifice. By appealing to people's deep emotional connection to their homeland, propagandists can convince them to put their lives on the line for the greater good. Patriotism is often tied to notions of heroism and honor, creating a narrative where soldiers become symbols of national pride.

One effective method of utilizing nationalism and patriotism is through symbols and imagery. Flags, national anthems, and other patriotic symbols are employed to evoke strong emotions and create a sense of unity. These symbols act as powerful triggers, reinforcing the narrative of national identity and fostering a sense of belonging. Propagandists also utilize powerful slogans and catchphrases that resonate with people's patriotic sentiments, further solidifying their allegiance.

Another strategy is to create a dichotomy between "us" and "them." By dehumanizing the enemy and emphasizing their differences, propagandists heighten nationalism and patriotism. This tactic fosters an "ingroup" mentality, where people feel a strong sense of camaraderie with fellow citizens and a desire to protect their shared values.

However, it is crucial to recognize the potential dangers of unchecked nationalism and blind patriotism. As consumers of war propaganda, people must be aware of manipulative techniques that exploit these emotions. By critically analyzing the messages presented to them, individuals can better understand the underlying motivations behind war propaganda and make informed decisions.

In conclusion, nationalism and patriotism are powerful tools in the arsenal of war propagandists. Understanding how these concepts are utilized allows people to critically evaluate the messages presented to them. By recognizing the psychological mechanisms at play, individuals can guard against manipulation and make informed choices about their support for military endeavors.

Chapter III

The Impact of War Propaganda on Public Opinion

Formation of Public Opinion through Propaganda

Propaganda is a powerful tool that has been extensively utilized throughout history to shape public opinion, particularly in the context of war. In the book "The Psychology of War Propaganda: How It Shapes Public Opinion," we delve into the intricate workings of this phenomenon and its profound effects on society. This subchapter aims to shed light on the formation of public opinion through the lens of war propaganda, offering valuable insights to people interested in understanding the intricate dynamics of this niche.

Public opinion plays a crucial role in determining the outcome of any conflict, and propaganda is a key instrument in influencing and manipulating it. By definition, propaganda is the dissemination of biased or misleading information, often with the intention of promoting a particular political agenda or viewpoint. During times of war, governments, militaries, and other entities employ propaganda techniques to sway public sentiment in their favor.

One of the most effective ways propaganda shapes public opinion is by appealing to emotions. Fear, anger, and patriotism are commonly exploited to evoke strong emotional responses, which can sway individuals' opinions and rally support for a particular cause. Through carefully crafted messages, images, and narratives, propagandists create a sense of urgency, instilling a belief that one's nation or cause is under threat, thus justifying any action taken.

Another powerful technique employed in war propaganda is the use of misinformation and manipulation of facts. By selectively presenting information or distorting the truth, propagandists can shape public perceptions and create a narrative that aligns with their objectives. This manipulation often involves demonizing the enemy, dehumanizing them, and exaggerating their crimes or intentions, creating a strong sense of "us versus them" mentality.

Furthermore, propaganda often relies on the power of repetition and widespread dissemination. By saturating various media channels, including newspapers, radio, television, and social media, propagandists ensure their messages reach a wide audience. Repetition reinforces key ideas, making them more likely to be accepted as truth, even without concrete evidence.

Understanding the formation of public opinion through war propaganda is crucial for anyone interested in comprehending the mechanics behind societal perceptions during times of conflict. By recognizing the techniques and strategies employed by propagandists, people can develop a critical mindset and become immune to manipulation. This knowledge empowers individuals to question the information they receive, verify facts, and form opinions based on a more accurate understanding of events.

In conclusion, the formation of public opinion through propaganda is a complex and fascinating subject. By exploring the various techniques employed in war propaganda, individuals can gain valuable insights into the shaping of public opinion and develop a more discerning approach towards the information presented to them. By understanding the power of propaganda, people can actively engage in conversations and debates, ensuring a more informed and democratic society.

Influence on Decision Making and Support for War Efforts

War propaganda has long been employed as a powerful tool to shape public opinion and garner support for military endeavors. Understanding the psychology behind this manipulation is crucial to comprehend how governments and organizations can sway the masses towards war. This subchapter delves into the intricate ways in which war propaganda influences decision-making processes and garners support for war efforts.

At its core, war propaganda aims to appeal to people's emotions and manipulate their cognitive processes. By tapping into deeply rooted fears, desires, and social identities, propaganda campaigns can effectively shape public opinion and generate support for military actions. One of the most prominent techniques employed is the creation of a perceived threat or enemy. By painting a vivid picture of an imminent danger, propaganda instills a sense of urgency and fear, compelling individuals to rally behind war efforts.

Moreover, war propaganda often employs various cognitive biases to sway decision-making. Confirmation bias, for instance, leads individuals to seek information that aligns with their preconceived notions, reinforcing their support for war efforts. Similarly, the availability heuristic can be exploited by presenting vivid and emotionally charged stories that easily come to mind, thus influencing people's perception of reality.

In addition to emotional manipulation and cognitive biases, war propaganda also targets specific niches within society. By tailoring messages to resonate with different groups, propaganda can effectively mobilize support from various demographics. For instance, messages emphasizing national pride might appeal to patriotic citizens, while narratives focusing on security may resonate with those concerned about personal safety. By understanding the unique needs and motivations of each niche, war propaganda can effectively influence decision-making processes and generate support.

It is essential for people to recognize the power and influence of war propaganda to maintain a critical and informed perspective. By being aware of the techniques employed, individuals can better evaluate and discern the validity of the messages they encounter. This subchapter aims to shed light on the intricate ways in which war propaganda shapes public opinion and influences decision-making processes. By understanding the psychological mechanisms at play, people can develop a more nuanced understanding of the role of propaganda in war efforts, allowing for a more informed and responsible engagement with the topic.

Psychological Effects on Individuals and Society

War propaganda is a powerful tool that has been utilized throughout history to shape public opinion and mobilize societies for war. Its impact, however, extends far beyond the realm of politics and military actions. In this subchapter, we will explore the profound psychological effects that war propaganda has on individuals and society as a whole.

At an individual level, war propaganda can have a significant impact on emotions, beliefs, and behaviors. Whether through subtle manipulation or overt indoctrination, propaganda can shape individuals' perceptions of the enemy, creating a dehumanizing effect that justifies violence and aggression. It can instill fear, anger, and hatred, leading individuals to support military actions and abandon critical thinking. Moreover, war propaganda often exploits individuals' sense of belonging and patriotism, fostering a strong desire to defend their nation and its ideals.

On a societal level, war propaganda can have far-reaching consequences. It can create a climate of fear and distrust, dividing communities and stifling dissent. Propaganda campaigns often rely on demonizing the enemy, creating an "us versus them" mentality that erodes empathy and tolerance. This can lead to increased xenophobia, discrimination, and even violence towards perceived enemies or minority groups.

Furthermore, war propaganda can impact society's collective memory and historical narrative. By controlling the information and shaping the narrative surrounding past conflicts, propaganda can shape how society remembers and interprets its own history. This can perpetuate biases, distort the truth, and hinder reconciliation and understanding between nations.

The psychological effects of war propaganda are not limited to times of active conflict. Even in times of peace, the residual effects of propaganda campaigns can linger, shaping attitudes and perceptions for years to come. The manipulation of public opinion can have long-lasting consequences on democracy, freedom of speech, and the ability to critically engage with complex geopolitical issues.

Understanding the psychological effects of war propaganda is crucial for individuals and society to guard against manipulation and maintain a healthy skepticism towards media messages. By developing critical thinking skills, fostering empathy, and promoting open dialogue, we can mitigate the negative impacts of war propaganda and work towards a more peaceful and informed world.

In conclusion, war propaganda has profound psychological effects on individuals and society. It manipulates emotions, beliefs, and behaviors, shaping public opinion and mobilizing societies for war. It can create division, fear, and hatred, leading to discrimination and violence. By recognizing and understanding these effects, we can strive for a more informed, empathetic, and peaceful society.

Chapter IV

Case Studies of War Propaganda Campaigns

World War I: The Power of Propaganda

Propaganda is a powerful tool that has been used throughout history to shape public opinion and influence the outcome of wars. In the context of World War I, propaganda played a crucial role in mobilizing the masses and rallying support for the war effort. This subchapter explores the various strategies employed by governments and military authorities during this tumultuous period, shedding light on the psychological aspects of war propaganda.

One of the key objectives of war propaganda during World War I was to create a sense of national unity and patriotism among the population. Governments utilized various mediums, such as posters, newspapers, and films, to disseminate their messages and evoke strong emotions in people. These propaganda materials often depicted heroic soldiers, valiantly fighting for their country, and portrayed the enemy as ruthless and inhumane. By appealing to people's emotions and sense of identity, propaganda instilled a deep sense of nationalism and encouraged individuals to support the war effort.

Another significant aspect of World War I propaganda was the demonization of the enemy. Governments employed dehumanizing tactics to portray the opposing forces as barbaric, bloodthirsty, and morally corrupt. These negative depictions aimed to generate fear and hatred towards the enemy, making it easier for the public to accept the necessity of war and justify the sacrifices being made.

Furthermore, propaganda was instrumental in shaping public opinion about the war's objectives. Governments employed persuasive language and imagery to convince people that the war was being fought for noble causes, such as freedom, democracy, or self-defense. By presenting the conflict as a just and righteous endeavor, propaganda aimed to garner support and maintain morale among the population.

However, it is crucial to recognize that propaganda is not a one-sided affair. The audience's susceptibility to propaganda played a significant role in its effectiveness. People's fears, hopes, and biases influenced their reception of propaganda messages. Understanding these psychological factors is vital in comprehending the power propaganda holds over public opinion.

In conclusion, the power of propaganda during World War I cannot be underestimated. It was a force that shaped public opinion, galvanized support, and influenced the outcome of the war. By exploiting psychological vulnerabilities and appealing to people's emotions, governments successfully controlled the narrative and mobilized entire nations. This subchapter delves into the multifaceted world of war propaganda, shedding light on its strategies, impact, and the role of the audience in its effectiveness. By understanding the power of propaganda, we gain insights into the psychological mechanisms that shape public opinion during times of conflict.

World War II: Propaganda on a Global Scale

Propaganda has always played a significant role in shaping public opinion during times of war. However, World War II took the use of propaganda to an entirely new level. With advancements in technology and communication, governments and military forces weaponized propaganda on a global scale to control the narrative, manipulate public opinion, and rally support for their respective causes.

During World War II, propaganda became more sophisticated, pervasive, and influential than ever before. Governments on all sides of the conflict recognized the power of propaganda in shaping public sentiment and utilized it to their advantage. They employed various mediums such as radio, newspapers, movies, posters, and even leaflets dropped from airplanes to disseminate their messages to the masses.

One of the most notable examples of wartime propaganda was the Nazi regime's use of it to promote their ideology and demonize their enemies. Adolf Hitler and his propagandist Joseph Goebbels employed a multifaceted approach to indoctrinate the German population and gain their unwavering support. The infamous German propaganda machine used powerful imagery, catchy slogans, and emotional appeals to manipulate public opinion and instill a sense of nationalistic pride and superiority.

Similarly, the Allied forces recognized the importance of propaganda in winning the hearts and minds of their citizens. They utilized films, posters, and radio broadcasts to convey messages of unity, bravery, and the importance of victory against the Axis powers. Propaganda was used to boost morale, encourage enlistment, and promote war bond sales to finance the war effort.

Beyond the home front, propaganda played a crucial role in shaping international perceptions of the war. Governments sought to gain support from neutral countries or sway their allegiance by portraying their own cause as just and their adversaries as evil. They disseminated information highlighting war crimes committed by the enemy, exaggerating their atrocities while downplaying their own.

However, propaganda during World War II was not limited to governments alone. Resistance movements and underground organizations also employed propaganda as a tool to rally their populations against occupation forces. Secret radio broadcasts, clandestine newspapers, and pamphlets were used to keep hope alive, disseminate information, and encourage acts of resistance.

World War II marked a turning point in the history of war propaganda. It demonstrated the power of psychological manipulation on a global scale and showcased the extent to which governments and military forces would go to shape public opinion. Understanding the tactics and impact of wartime propaganda allows us to critically analyze historical events and be more discerning consumers of information in today's media-saturated world.

Cold War Era: The Battle for Hearts and Minds

In the midst of the Cold War, a new form of warfare emerged, one that did not involve bullets or tanks but instead focused on the manipulation of public opinion. This subchapter explores the fascinating world of war propaganda during the Cold War era and its profound impact on shaping the hearts and minds of people across the globe.

The Cold War was a highly tense political and ideological standoff between the United States and the Soviet Union that lasted from the end of World War II until the early 1990s. Both superpowers recognized the power of propaganda as a tool to win the hearts and minds of their citizens and the international community. This battle for public opinion became a critical part of the overall conflict, as each side sought to establish dominance in the minds of the people.

War propaganda during the Cold War era took many forms. Governments utilized various mediums such as newspapers, radio broadcasts, posters, and films to disseminate their messages. The United States, for example, employed renowned artists and writers to create captivating propaganda pieces that promoted American values and painted the Soviet Union as a threat to freedom and democracy. On the other side, the Soviet Union used propaganda to promote the idea of a utopian communist society and vilify the capitalist West.

One of the most effective tools of war propaganda during this era was the use of fear. Both superpowers sought to instill fear in their own citizens and the citizens of other nations, emphasizing the potential catastrophic consequences of their enemy's ideology. The threat of nuclear war loomed large, and propaganda campaigns exploited this fear to their advantage.

The battle for hearts and minds during the Cold War era not only targeted the citizens of the superpowers but also aimed to influence people in other countries. Both sides sought to gain allies and supporters by portraying themselves as the champions of justice and freedom. Propaganda campaigns were carefully crafted to appeal to the emotions and values of different cultures, exploiting existing divisions and tensions.

The impact of war propaganda during the Cold War era cannot be overstated. It shaped public opinion, influenced policy decisions, and ultimately played a significant role in the outcome of the Cold War. Understanding the psychological mechanisms behind war propaganda is crucial to recognizing its enduring effects on societies today.

In conclusion, the Cold War era was marked by a fierce battle for hearts and minds through the use of war propaganda. This subchapter has explored the various forms and strategies employed by both the United States and the Soviet Union during this era. By dissecting the psychological tactics used, we can better understand how war propaganda shaped public opinion and influenced the outcome of this monumental conflict.

Modern Propaganda: The Digital Age

Introduction: In today's interconnected world, the influence of propaganda has reached unprecedented heights. With the advent of the digital age, propaganda techniques have evolved and adapted to the ever-changing landscape of online platforms and social media. This subchapter explores the impact of modern propaganda in shaping public opinion in the context of war propaganda.

Propaganda in the Digital Era: The digital age has transformed the way information is disseminated, creating new opportunities and challenges for propagandists. The ease of access to information, coupled with the rapid spread of content online, has allowed propaganda to infiltrate every aspect of our lives. Today, war propaganda has become more subtle, pervasive, and personalized, making it increasingly difficult for individuals to discern fact from fiction.

Social Media and Propaganda: Social media platforms have become breeding grounds for propaganda, providing a vast network for disseminating messages to target audiences. By leveraging algorithms and user data, propagandists can tailor content to specific demographics, amplifying confirmation bias and reinforcing pre-existing beliefs. The viral nature of social media further magnifies the impact of propaganda, enabling its rapid spread and potential to influence public opinion on a global scale.

Manipulating Emotions: Modern propaganda has perfected the art of emotional manipulation. Through carefully crafted narratives, propagandists exploit human vulnerabilities, tapping into fear, anger, and empathy to shape public opinion. By leveraging emotionally charged content, such as graphic images or heart-wrenching stories, propagandists can sway individuals towards their desired agenda, further polarizing society and fueling conflicts.

Disinformation and Fake News: The digital age has witnessed the proliferation of disinformation and fake news, making it increasingly challenging to differentiate truth from falsehoods. Propagandists exploit this vulnerability by disseminating false narratives, misleading images, and fabricated stories. With the help of technology, deep fakes and AI-generated content have further blurred the lines between reality and fiction, making it crucial for individuals to critically evaluate the information they encounter.

Countering Modern Propaganda: As individuals, it is essential to develop a media literacy toolkit to navigate the treacherous waters of modern propaganda. Fact-checking, cross-referencing sources, and critical thinking are vital tools in identifying and countering propaganda.

Governments, media organizations, and tech giants also bear the responsibility of implementing policies and technologies to curb the spread of misinformation and ensure transparency in the digital realm.

Conclusion: In the digital age, modern propaganda has become an omnipresent force with the potential to shape public opinion on a massive scale. The interplay between technology, social media, and human psychology has given rise to a new era of propaganda. Understanding these dynamics and developing critical thinking skills are essential for individuals to navigate the digital landscape and safeguard themselves against the manipulation of war propaganda.

Chapter V

Ethical Considerations in War Propaganda

The Ethics of Manipulating Public Opinion

In the world of war propaganda, a topic of great significance and concern arises: the ethics of manipulating public opinion. As people, it is essential for us to critically examine the methods employed by war propagandists in shaping our perceptions, beliefs, and attitudes towards conflicts. This subchapter delves into the ethical implications of such manipulations, urging readers interested in the niche of war propaganda to reflect upon their role as informed citizens.

Manipulating public opinion during times of war is a powerful tool that can be used for both noble and sinister purposes. While some argue that it is justifiable to sway public sentiment in support of a righteous cause, others contend that any form of manipulation undermines the principles of truth, honesty, and autonomy. The ethical dilemma lies in determining when the ends justify the means.

One key consideration is the potential for harm. When war propaganda is used to vilify an enemy or distort facts, it can lead to a dehumanization of the "other," fostering an environment of fear, hatred, and hostility. This can not only escalate conflicts but also perpetuate cycles of violence and result in the mistreatment of innocent civilians. As consumers of war propaganda, we must question whether we are willing to accept the potential harm caused by manipulative tactics.

Another ethical concern revolves around the concept of informed consent. Manipulating public opinion often involves withholding or distorting information, depriving individuals of the ability to make informed decisions. By carefully selecting which facts to disclose and how to frame them, war propagandists can sway public opinion in their favor. This raises questions about the fundamental right of individuals to access accurate and unbiased information, and the potential consequences of a society lacking informed citizens.

Furthermore, the ethical implications of manipulating public opinion extend to the erosion of trust in institutions and the media. When individuals become aware of manipulative tactics, they may develop skepticism and cynicism towards all information presented to them. This erosion of trust can have far-reaching consequences for the functioning of a democratic society, as it undermines the ability to engage in informed debates and make collective decisions.

In conclusion, the ethics of manipulating public opinion in the realm of war propaganda is a multifaceted and complex issue. As people interested in the niche of war propaganda, we must grapple with questions surrounding harm, informed consent, and the erosion of trust. By critically examining the methods employed and the potential consequences, we can foster a more informed and ethically conscious society.

Balancing National Security and Information Transparency

Subchapter: Balancing National Security and Information Transparency

In the realm of war propaganda, a delicate balance must be struck between national security and information transparency. In this subchapter, we delve into the complex dynamics that underlie this delicate equilibrium and explore its consequences on public opinion. By understanding this balance, we can gain valuable insight into the psychology of war propaganda and its impact on society.

In times of conflict, governments are faced with the challenging task of protecting national security while simultaneously ensuring that the public remains informed about the realities of war. This task is not an easy one, as too much transparency can compromise military strategies and endanger the lives of soldiers and civilians, while excessive secrecy can breed distrust and skepticism among the public.

The relationship between national security and information transparency is a delicate dance, requiring governments to carefully navigate the fine line between withholding sensitive information and maintaining public trust. War propaganda plays a pivotal role in this delicate balance, as it shapes public opinion and influences the perception of national security.

War propaganda is a powerful tool that governments use to manipulate public sentiment, often by selectively presenting information that aligns with their own objectives. Through the strategic dissemination of information, governments can control the narrative and shape public opinion to garner support for their military endeavors. This manipulation can be particularly potent during times of crisis, when emotions are heightened, and critical thinking may be compromised.

However, striking the right balance is essential to prevent the erosion of public trust. Citizens have a fundamental right to know the truth, and excessive secrecy can breed suspicion and skepticism. When governments are perceived as withholding information or manipulating the truth, public trust can diminish, leading to a breakdown in societal cohesion and potential backlash against military actions.

To maintain this balance, governments must engage in responsible information sharing. They should provide accurate and timely updates on military operations while safeguarding sensitive information that could compromise national security. Transparent communication can foster trust and ensure that the public feels adequately informed without jeopardizing strategic interests.

In conclusion, the delicate balance between national security and information transparency is a crucial aspect of war propaganda. Governments must navigate this fine line carefully to maintain public trust while safeguarding national security. By understanding the psychological dynamics at play, we can critically evaluate war propaganda and its impact on public opinion. Ultimately, it is the responsibility of both governments and citizens to strive for a balance that upholds the principles of democracy and ensures informed decision-making in times of conflict.

Responsibility of Governments and Media Outlets

In the realm of war propaganda, the responsibility of governments and media outlets cannot be overstated. This subchapter delves into the crucial role these entities play in shaping public opinion during times of conflict. Understanding their responsibilities is vital for individuals interested in war propaganda and its psychological impact on society.

Governments hold a significant responsibility when it comes to war propaganda. As the primary orchestrators of military campaigns, they have the power to manipulate information and shape narratives to achieve their objectives. However, this power must be wielded responsibly, as the consequences of misinformation or manipulation can be severe. Governments must prioritize accurate reporting, transparency, and ethical communication to ensure citizens are well-informed.

Media outlets, as the intermediaries between governments and the public, also bear immense responsibility. Journalists and news organizations play a pivotal role in disseminating information to the masses. They must strive for objectivity and unbiased reporting, enabling citizens to form informed opinions. However, media outlets often face challenges in maintaining their independence, especially during times of war. Pressure from governments, economic interests, and ideological biases can influence their coverage, potentially leading to the propagation of propaganda.

To fulfill their responsibilities, governments and media outlets must adhere to certain principles. Governments should prioritize the protection of press freedom, allowing journalists to report on conflicts without fear of retribution. They should support initiatives that promote media literacy, enabling citizens to critically analyze news sources. Governments must also commit to transparency, providing timely and accurate information to the public.

Media outlets, on the other hand, must uphold journalistic ethics and prioritize fact-checking. They should diversify their sources of information, providing a comprehensive view of the conflict. Media organizations should also engage in self-regulation, holding themselves accountable for their coverage and addressing any biases or inaccuracies.

The responsibility of governments and media outlets extends beyond their actions during wartime. They must also focus on post-conflict periods, facilitating reconciliation and fostering a culture of peace. This involves promoting dialogue, challenging divisive narratives, and supporting efforts to rebuild trust among different communities affected by conflict.

In conclusion, the responsibility of governments and media outlets in war propaganda is immense. Both entities must prioritize accuracy, transparency, and ethical communication to ensure citizens are well-informed. Upholding these principles can help mitigate the psychological impact of war propaganda and contribute to a more informed and peaceful society.

Chapter VI

Countering War Propaganda

Promoting Media Literacy and Critical Thinking

In today's fast-paced world, where information bombards us from every angle, it has become crucial to develop media literacy and critical thinking skills. These skills are particularly vital when it comes to understanding the impact of war propaganda on public opinion. In this subchapter, we will explore the importance of media literacy and critical thinking in deciphering the workings of war propaganda and its influence on society.

War propaganda has long been used as a powerful tool to shape public opinion, manipulate emotions, and rally support for military endeavors. However, by promoting media literacy, individuals can become more discerning consumers of information and less susceptible to the influence of propaganda. Media literacy enables people to critically analyze the messages they receive, identify biases, and distinguish between objective reporting and propaganda.

Critical thinking plays a significant role in developing media literacy. By questioning the underlying motives and agendas behind the information presented, individuals can better understand the potential biases and manipulations at play. Critical thinkers are not easily swayed by emotional appeals or misleading narratives, but instead, seek evidence, evaluate sources, and consider multiple perspectives before forming their opinions.

This chapter will provide readers with practical strategies to enhance media literacy and critical thinking skills. We will delve into techniques for analyzing media content, such as fact-checking, cross-referencing sources, and recognizing logical fallacies. Additionally, we will explore the psychological tactics employed in war propaganda, such as emotional manipulation, demonization of the enemy, and the use of catchy slogans or images.

Moreover, we will highlight the importance of independent research and seeking information from diverse sources. By expanding our media consumption beyond a single outlet or perspective, we can gain a more comprehensive understanding of complex issues, challenge our own biases, and avoid falling victim to the echo chamber effect.

Ultimately, this subchapter aims to empower people with the tools to navigate the intricate world of war propaganda, fostering critical thinking and media literacy. By developing these skills, individuals can become active participants in shaping public opinion, resist manipulation, and make informed decisions about war and conflict. With media literacy and critical thinking as our allies, we can strive for a more enlightened and aware society, capable of distinguishing between truth and propaganda.

Alternative Narratives and Independent Journalism

In today's world of information overload, where news is often distorted or manipulated to serve various agendas, the need for alternative narratives and independent journalism has become more crucial than ever before. In this subchapter, we will explore the importance of seeking alternative perspectives and the role of independent journalism in countering the effects of war propaganda.

War propaganda has long been used as a powerful tool to shape public opinion and justify military actions. Governments and powerful entities have historically controlled the narrative, suppressing dissenting voices and manipulating the information available to the public. However, the rise of independent journalism has provided a glimmer of hope amidst this sea of misinformation.

Independent journalism refers to news organizations or individuals who are not influenced by political or corporate interests. They strive to present unbiased, factual information and give voice to marginalized perspectives that are often ignored by mainstream media. By seeking alternative narratives, independent journalism challenges the dominant war propaganda and encourages critical thinking among the public.

One of the key benefits of alternative narratives and independent journalism is their ability to expose the hidden agendas behind war propaganda. They shed light on the discrepancies between what is being reported and the reality on the ground. By presenting multiple viewpoints, independent journalism allows people to form a more comprehensive understanding of complex conflicts, going beyond the simplistic narratives often presented by propagandists.

Moreover, alternative narratives and independent journalism empower individuals to question the official narratives and seek the truth. They encourage citizens to become active participants in the information ecosystem, rather than passive consumers of propaganda. By promoting transparency and accountability, independent journalism fosters a more informed and engaged public, capable of making well-informed decisions.

However, it is important to acknowledge the challenges faced by independent journalists. They often operate in hostile environments, facing censorship, intimidation, and even violence. As consumers of news, we must support independent journalism by seeking out alternative sources, subscribing to independent news outlets, and advocating for press freedom.

By embracing alternative narratives and independent journalism, we can break free from the shackles of war propaganda and develop a more nuanced understanding of conflicts. We can become critical thinkers who are not easily swayed by one-sided narratives. Ultimately, by empowering ourselves with diverse perspectives, we can contribute to a more peaceful and just society.

In conclusion, alternative narratives and independent journalism play a crucial role in countering the effects of war propaganda. They challenge dominant narratives, expose hidden agendas, and empower individuals to seek the truth. By supporting independent journalism, we can foster a more informed and engaged public, capable of making well-informed decisions. Let us embrace alternative narratives and independent journalism as tools to dismantle the machinery of war propaganda and pave the way for a more balanced and just world.

Public Awareness and Grassroots Movements

In the world of war propaganda, public awareness and grassroots movements play a crucial role in shaping public opinion. The power of information dissemination is immense, and understanding its psychological impact is essential in today's society. This subchapter delves into the importance of public awareness and grassroots movements in the context of war propaganda, aiming to shed light on how they influence the perception of conflict.

Public awareness serves as a critical tool in war propaganda, as it allows governments and influential entities to sway public opinion in favor of their own agenda. By carefully crafting messages and disseminating them through various media channels, these entities can mold public perception and generate support for their military endeavors. Understanding the psychology behind this manipulation is crucial for people to recognize and critically evaluate the information presented to them.

Grassroots movements, on the other hand, offer a counterbalance to the controlled narrative of war propaganda. These movements arise from the collective voices of ordinary people who challenge the dominant discourse and seek to expose hidden truths. Grassroots movements often utilize social media platforms, public demonstrations, and alternative media sources to spread their messages, aiming to raise public awareness and counter the influence of war propaganda.

By actively encouraging public awareness and supporting grassroots movements, people can become agents of change in the face of war propaganda. They can question the information presented to them, seek alternative perspectives, and engage in dialogue to foster a more informed society. This subchapter explores the various strategies individuals can employ to develop critical thinking skills and resist the influence of war propaganda.

Moreover, it highlights the importance of media literacy, encouraging people to analyze the motives and biases behind news sources. By understanding the techniques used in war propaganda, individuals can better decipher the underlying messages and make well-informed decisions.

In conclusion, public awareness and grassroots movements are pivotal in shaping public opinion amidst the realm of war propaganda. By fostering critical thinking skills, questioning information, and supporting alternative voices, individuals can resist the manipulation of war propaganda and contribute to a more informed and discerning society. It is only through a collective effort to raise public awareness that we can challenge the dominant narrative and strive for a more peaceful world.

Chapter VII

The Future of War Propaganda

Technological Advancements and Evolving Tactics

In the realm of war propaganda, technological advancements have played a significant role in shaping public opinion. The interplay between evolving tactics and the utilization of cutting-edge technology has resulted in a dynamic landscape of psychological warfare. Understanding these advancements is crucial for people interested in war propaganda and its effects on public opinion.

One of the most notable technological advancements in recent times is the rise of social media platforms. These platforms have revolutionized the dissemination of information, making it easier for governments and organizations to spread their narratives to the masses. With the ability to reach millions in an instant, social media has become an influential tool in shaping public opinion during times of conflict. Governments now have the power to control the narrative, manipulate information, and even amplify the voices of their supporters while suppressing dissenting opinions.

Additionally, advancements in data analytics and artificial intelligence have enabled more sophisticated targeting of propaganda messages. Through the analysis of vast amounts of user data, advertisers, political organizations, and even governments can tailor their messages to specific demographics, further reinforcing their desired narratives. This personalized approach to propaganda has proven highly effective in influencing public opinion, as individuals are more likely to engage with content that aligns with their beliefs and values.

Furthermore, technological advancements have not only influenced the dissemination of propaganda but also the tactics employed during warfare. For instance, the use of unmanned aerial vehicles, commonly known as drones, has revolutionized modern warfare. Drones offer governments the ability to conduct precision strikes without putting their soldiers' lives at risk. However, their use also raises ethical and moral questions, as well as concerns about civilian casualties. War propaganda often seeks to justify the use of such technology by framing it as a necessary measure in the pursuit of national security.

As technology continues to advance, so too will the tactics employed in war propaganda. It is crucial for people interested in this field to stay informed and critically analyze the information they consume. By understanding the evolving tactics and technological advancements, individuals can better navigate the complex landscape of war propaganda and its impact on public opinion.

In conclusion, the subchapter on "Technological Advancements and Evolving Tactics" sheds light on the crucial role technology plays in war propaganda and its influence on public opinion. The rise of social media, advancements in data analytics and artificial intelligence, and the utilization of cutting-edge military technology have transformed the way governments and organizations shape narratives during times of conflict. As people interested in war propaganda, it is essential to be aware of these advancements and their potential impact on public opinion. By critically analyzing the information we consume and staying informed, we can navigate the ever-changing landscape of war propaganda more effectively.

Potential Impact of Artificial Intelligence and Big Data

In the digital age, the convergence of Artificial Intelligence (AI) and Big Data has unleashed unprecedented possibilities across various sectors, and war propaganda is no exception. The potential impact of AI and Big Data on the realm of war propaganda is both intriguing and concerning. This subchapter aims to shed light on the implications of these technologies on shaping public opinion in the context of warfare.

Artificial Intelligence, with its ability to analyze vast amounts of data and make autonomous decisions, has the potential to revolutionize the field of war propaganda. AI algorithms can sift through enormous volumes of information, ranging from social media posts to news articles, to identify patterns and sentiments. This enables governments and military organizations to tailor their propaganda campaigns to specific target audiences, amplifying messages that resonate with their ideologies or objectives.

Moreover, AI can automate the creation of persuasive content, including text, images, and videos, making it increasingly difficult for individuals to distinguish between authentic and fabricated information. This blurring of lines can significantly impact public opinion, as people may unknowingly consume and support propaganda that aligns with the interests of those employing AI-generated content.

Big Data, on the other hand, provides a treasure trove of information that can be harnessed to influence public sentiment. By analyzing vast datasets, governments and propagandists can identify trends, preferences, and vulnerabilities within specific populations. This knowledge allows them to craft propaganda campaigns that exploit psychological biases and manipulate emotions, ultimately swaying public opinion in favor of their agendas.

However, the potential impact of AI and Big Data on war propaganda raises significant ethical concerns. The use of AI to deceive or manipulate individuals undermines the principles of democracy and freedom of thought. The indiscriminate dissemination of misinformation and propaganda erodes trust in institutions, sowing discord and potentially inciting violence.

Additionally, the reliance on AI and Big Data in war propaganda poses challenges for accountability and transparency. As AI algorithms become more complex and self-learning, it becomes increasingly difficult to trace the origins and intentions of propaganda materials. This lack of transparency limits society's ability to critically evaluate information and make informed decisions.

In conclusion, the potential impact of Artificial Intelligence and Big Data on war propaganda is immense. While these technologies offer unprecedented opportunities for tailored messaging and data-driven influence, the ethical implications cannot be disregarded. It is crucial for individuals, governments, and organizations to critically engage with these advancements, ensuring that the power of

AI and Big Data is harnessed responsibly and ethically to protect the integrity of public opinion and democratic values.

Mitigating the Harmful Effects of Future Propaganda

Introduction:

In the era of information overload, war propaganda has become an insidious tool that shapes public opinion and influences the course of conflicts. The power of propaganda lies in its ability to manipulate emotions, distort reality, and manipulate individuals into supporting actions they might otherwise reject. Understanding the psychology behind war propaganda is crucial for people, especially those interested in the niche of war propaganda, to protect themselves from its harmful effects. This subchapter aims to provide insights into mitigating the impact of future propaganda.

1. Developing Media Literacy:

In the age of digital media, it is essential for people to develop media literacy skills. By critically analyzing news sources, fact-checking information, and understanding the biases that exist, individuals can become more immune to the influence of propaganda. Educating people about media manipulation techniques, such as framing and emotional appeal, can empower them to recognize and resist propaganda efforts.

2. Encouraging Critical Thinking:

Promoting critical thinking is paramount to mitigating the harmful effects of propaganda. By encouraging people to question information, seek multiple perspectives, and evaluate evidence, they can cultivate a healthy skepticism towards propaganda. Schools, universities, and community organizations should incorporate critical thinking education into their curriculum to equip individuals with the necessary skills to navigate the complex landscape of war propaganda.

3. Promoting Diversity and Inclusion:

Propaganda often targets specific groups by exploiting existing biases and divisions. By fostering diversity and inclusion, people can create an environment that is less susceptible to propaganda. Embracing different perspectives, encouraging dialogue, and promoting empathy can help bridge divides and reduce the effectiveness of propaganda in manipulating public opinion.

4. Building Resilience against Emotional Manipulation:

Propaganda relies heavily on appealing to emotions such as fear, anger, and patriotism. Building emotional resilience can shield individuals from falling prey to emotional manipulation. By promoting emotional intelligence, mindfulness, and self-awareness, people can recognize when their emotions are being exploited and make rational decisions based on facts rather than manipulated sentiment.

Conclusion:

Mitigating the harmful effects of future war propaganda requires a collective effort from individuals, communities, and institutions. By fostering media literacy, critical thinking, diversity, and emotional resilience, people can protect themselves and their communities from the insidious influence of propaganda. Understanding the psychology behind war propaganda is the first step towards empowering individuals and shaping a more informed and resistant society.

Chapter VIII

Conclusion

Recap of Key Findings

In this subchapter, we will provide a comprehensive recap of the key findings discussed throughout this book, "The Psychology of War Propaganda: How It Shapes Public Opinion." This book aims to shed light on the intricate workings of war propaganda and its profound impact on public perception. Our audience, people interested in war propaganda, will find this recap immensely valuable in understanding the core concepts and insights explored in this book.

Throughout our exploration, we have discovered several essential findings that highlight the power and influence of war propaganda. Firstly, we have learned that war propaganda is a deliberate and systematic effort by governments and other influential entities to shape public opinion in times of conflict. It utilizes various psychological techniques to manipulate emotions, beliefs, and behaviors, ultimately shaping public support or opposition towards a particular war effort.

Moreover, we have examined the psychological mechanisms that make war propaganda so effective.

These mechanisms include the use of fear, demonization of the enemy, and the creation of a sense of national unity. By understanding these tactics, people can become more aware of the subtle ways in which war propaganda can impact their thoughts and actions.

Furthermore, we have explored the role of media in disseminating war propaganda. The media plays a crucial role in perpetuating and amplifying the messages of war propaganda, often without critically questioning their veracity. This highlights the importance of media literacy and critical thinking skills in deciphering the true motives behind the information presented to us.

Importantly, we have also delved into the ethical implications of war propaganda. By understanding the manipulative techniques employed, people can better evaluate the ethicality of the messages they encounter and make informed decisions regarding their support or opposition to war efforts.

In conclusion, this subchapter's recap of key findings provides a concise overview of the insights gained from "The Psychology of War Propaganda: How It Shapes Public Opinion." By understanding the deliberate techniques employed by war propagandists and the psychological mechanisms underlying their effectiveness, people interested in war propaganda can be more discerning consumers of information. Armed with this knowledge, they can critically evaluate the messages they encounter and become active participants in shaping public opinion, ultimately contributing to a more informed and aware society.

Implications for Society and Democracy

In today's world, where information is readily available and easily disseminated, the role of war propaganda in shaping public opinion cannot be underestimated. This subchapter delves into the implications that war propaganda has on society and democracy, shedding light on the profound impact it has on our collective psyche.

War propaganda has a dual effect on society, both uniting and dividing communities. On one hand, it serves as a unifying force, rallying citizens around a common cause or enemy. It instills a sense of patriotism and national identity, fostering a shared purpose and mobilizing support for war efforts. However, on the other hand, war propaganda can also create divisions within society. By demonizing the enemy and presenting a black-and-white narrative, it often exacerbates existing prejudices and fosters an "us versus them" mentality. This can lead to the dehumanization of the enemy, eroding empathy and promoting hostility between different groups, both domestically and internationally.

Furthermore, the impact of war propaganda on democracy is far-reaching. In a democratic society, an informed and critical citizenry is vital for the functioning of a healthy democracy. However, war propaganda can manipulate public opinion, stifling dissenting voices and limiting the diversity of perspectives. By controlling the narrative and framing the discourse, those in power can shape public opinion to suit their agenda, potentially undermining the democratic process. This concentration of power in the hands of a few threatens the principles of transparency, accountability, and pluralism that are the bedrock of any democratic society.

Moreover, war propaganda can have long-lasting psychological effects on individuals and society as a whole. It can induce fear, anxiety, and a heightened state of alertness, leading to a willingness to sacrifice civil liberties in exchange for security. It can also perpetuate stereotypes and fuel prejudices, further fragmenting society and hindering social cohesion. The psychological impact of war propaganda can be particularly pronounced on vulnerable individuals, such as children and those with pre-existing trauma, making them more susceptible to manipulation and indoctrination.

In conclusion, war propaganda has profound implications for society and democracy. By analyzing the role it plays in shaping public opinion, we can better understand its impact on our collective consciousness. Awareness of the potential pitfalls of war propaganda is essential to safeguarding democratic values and fostering a more informed and resilient society. It is crucial that we remain vigilant and critically evaluate the information we consume, ensuring that our opinions are not swayed by manipulative tactics.

Call to Action: Promoting a More Informed Public.

In today's world, where war propaganda plays a significant role in shaping public opinion, it is crucial for us as individuals to be more discerning and informed about the messages we receive. The power of war propaganda lies in its ability to manipulate our emotions, sway our beliefs, and ultimately influence our actions. As people interested in the topic of war propaganda, we have a responsibility to promote a more informed public, capable of critically analyzing and understanding the messages they encounter.

To achieve this goal, we must first acknowledge the pervasive nature of war propaganda in our society. It is not limited to overt advertisements or government-sponsored campaigns; it can be found in news outlets, social media, and even interpersonal conversations. We must develop a keen eye for recognizing the subtle tactics employed by propagandists, including emotional appeals, selective presentation of facts, and demonization of the enemy.

Education is the key to combating war propaganda and fostering a more informed public. We need to invest in teaching critical thinking skills, media literacy, and the ability to recognize biases. By equipping ourselves and others with these tools, we can empower individuals to question, challenge, and seek multiple perspectives before forming their own opinions.

In addition to personal education, it is crucial to engage in open dialogue and encourage diverse viewpoints. By actively seeking out different perspectives, we can broaden our understanding of complex issues and avoid falling into the trap of echo chambers. This includes engaging with individuals who may hold opposing views, as it is through respectful debate and discussion that we can dismantle misinformation and foster a more nuanced understanding of war propaganda.

As consumers of media, we must also support independent and reliable sources of information. By promoting ethical journalism and seeking out diverse sources, we can counter the dominance of biased narratives that often perpetuate war propaganda. This may involve subscribing to reputable news outlets, fact-checking information before sharing it, and supporting organizations that prioritize transparency and accuracy.

Ultimately, promoting a more informed public is a collective effort that requires individual commitment and societal change. By taking action to educate ourselves, engage in open dialogue, and support reliable sources of information, we can counter the influence of war propaganda and contribute to a more informed and empowered society. Let us rise above the manipulation and strive for a world where public opinion is shaped by critical thinking, empathy, and a genuine pursuit of truth.

May our understanding of the psychology of war propaganda lead us towards a future where knowledge triumphs over deception, and where the power of empathy prevails over the allure of division.